Weston Intermediate S
95 School Road
Weston, CT 06883

S0-AYI-421

FLOATING · SINKING

THE LEARNING RESOURCE CENTER
Weston Intermediate School

A Buddy Book

by

Julie Murray

ABDO
Publishing Company

VISIT US AT
www.abdopublishing.com

Published by ABDO Publishing Company, 4940 Viking Drive, Edina, Minnesota 55435.

Copyright © 2007 by Abdo Consulting Group, Inc. International copyrights reserved in all countries. No part of this book may be reproduced in any form without written permission from the publisher. Buddy Books™ is a trademark and logo of ABDO Publishing Company.

Printed in the United States.

Series Coordinator: Sarah Tieck
Contributing Editor: Michael P. Goecke
Graphic Design: Maria Hosley
Cover Photograph: Media Bakery
Interior Photographs/Illustrations: Clipart.com, Media Bakery, Photos.com

Library of Congress Cataloging-in-Publication Data

Murray, Julie, 1969–
    Floating and sinking / Julie Murray.
        p. cm. — (First science)
    Includes index.
    ISBN-13: 978-1-59679-823-6
    ISBN-10: 1-59679-823-8
    1. Floating bodies—Juvenile literature. 2. Hydrostatics—Juvenile literature. 3. Buoyant ascent (Hydrodynamics)—Juvenile literature. I. Title. II. Series: Murray, Julie, 1969- First science.

QC147.5.M87 2006
532'.25—dc22
                                                                2006017158

TABLE OF CONTENTS

SINKING INTO THE FACTS

Floating and sinking are a big part of everyday life. It is easy to see floating and sinking happening in many places.

Just look around! Boats float on lakes. Pennies sink to the bottom of fountains. And when people go to a swimming pool, they can float or sink in the water.

There are many examples of floating and sinking in daily life.

THE SCIENCE OF FLOATING AND SINKING

Some items float and some items sink. **Buoyancy** describes how well an object floats. Boats are buoyant. So are some bars of soap. Apples and pieces of wood are buoyant, too.

Buoys are buoyant objects. So people use them to mark waterways and protect their boats.

Logs are buoyant. So, people use rivers to transport them.

In the 200s BC, Greek **mathematician** Archimedes studied **buoyancy**. While he was taking a bath, he made a discovery about water. When he got into the bath, some of the water overflowed. His body had caused the liquid to push away. This is called **displacement**.

Archimedes came up with a scientific **theory** to explain what had happened. He said, "A floating object **displaces** an amount of liquid equal to its own weight." Today, this theory is called Archimedes' Principle.

Archimedes was a mathematician and a physicist.

WHAT FLOATS AND WHAT SINKS?

The key to understanding why an object can float is learning about **density**. Density refers to an object's weight and size.

Two objects that weigh the same can be different sizes. The smaller object is more dense. The larger object is less dense.

This boy and this stack of weights are about the same weight. This is possible because of density.

Objects that are more **dense** than a liquid will sink. If objects are less dense than a liquid, they will float.

The rocks are at the bottom of the fish bowl because they are more dense than the water.

This beach ball is less dense than water, so it floats.

Boats are able to float on the water. This is because of their shape. The air inside the boat allows it to float on water.

But, a boat sinks when it gets a hole in it. This is because water replaces the air in the boat. So the boat becomes more **dense**.

Most of a boat floats above the surface. But, a small part of the boat stays underwater. This displaces liquid.

A boat with a hole sinks as it fills with water.

FLOATING THROUGH HISTORY

Through the years, many scientists have tried to understand the science of floating and sinking.

The famous phrase, "Eureka! I have found it!" came from Archimedes.

In early times, Greek **mathematician** Archimedes worked hard to explain floating and sinking. He knew a lot about mathematics and science. And he was always experimenting with **formulas** and **theories**. Eventually, he became famous for his ideas about **buoyancy.** Today Archimedes' Principle is still important to the science of floating and sinking.

Since Archimedes' experiments long ago, many people have studied floating and sinking. And, they have made many important discoveries about this science. Still, most agree there is more to learn about floating and sinking.

Floating and sinking can also take place outside of water. A hot air balloon floats when the air trapped in the balloon is heated. The balloon sinks when the air is cooled.

FLOATING AND SINKING IN THE WORLD TODAY

Floating and sinking are a part of daily life. Without the ability to float, boats wouldn't be able to move through water. And, without the ability to sink, anchors could not be used to stop boats.

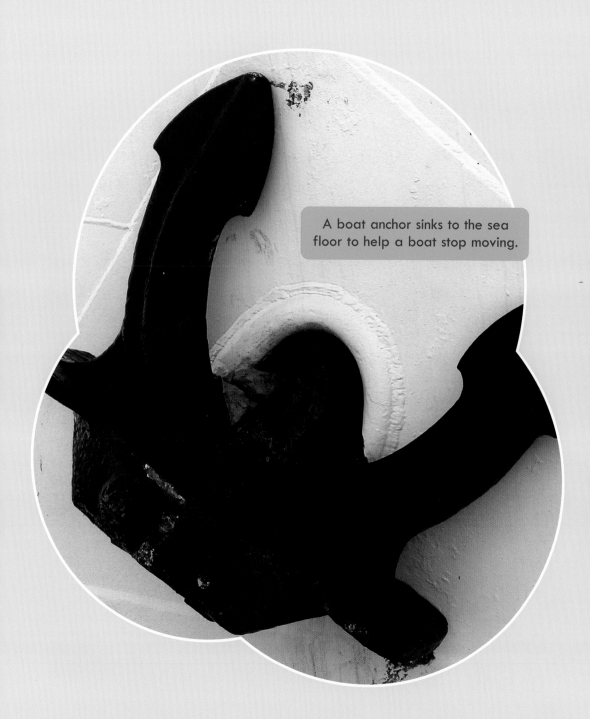

A boat anchor sinks to the sea floor to help a boat stop moving.

People can travel by sea because boats float and move on water.

The world would be a very different place if objects were not able to float or sink.

.. IMPORTANT WORDS ..

buoyancy an object's tendency to float.

density a description of an object's weight and size.

displace to replace or take the place of something else.

formula an explanation on how something works.

mathematics a person who studies numbers and amounts.

theory an explanation of how or why something happens.

.■ WEB SITES ■.

To learn more about **Floating and Sinking**, visit ABDO Publishing Company on the World Wide Web. Web site links about **Floating and Sinking** are featured on our Book Links page. These links are routinely monitored and updated to provide the most current information available.

www.abdopublishing.com

.·■ INDEX ■·.